Cheechako Grilled Salmon Steak

1½	lbs. salmon steaks		2	Tbsp. lemon or lime juice
3	cloves garlic, minced		1	tsp. salt
3	Tbsp. olive oil		1	tsp. fresh ground pepper
3	tsp. cajun seasoning		•	lemon wedges for garnish

Mix all marinade ingredients and pour over salmon steaks. Allow steaks to marinate for 1 hour. Place fillets over medium hot coals. Grill for 3 to 4 minutes on each side. Remove and serve with picnic potatoes and fresh garden vegetables. Yield: 4 servings.

nglers have an ongoing love affair with Alaska. Its fertile waters, world-renown for salmon, are home to an abundance of fish including trout, halibut, pollock and sea bass. Plentiful waters aside, the best thing about fishing Alaska is Alaska herself. Few places on earth behold such unforgettable beauty.

Alaskan Style Halibut Tacos

1½ lbs. halibut, cut into bite size pieces	1 bunch green onions, diced
1 pkg. taco seasoning	1 lb. Cheddar cheese, shredded
1 head lettuce	1 carton (8 oz.) sour cream
1 tomato, diced	18 taco shells

Place halibut in a non-stick skillet with ¼ cup water. Steam fish in water until it begins to flake. Add taco seasoning, cover and simmer for 2 minutes.

Supreme Basil Salmon

1-1½ lbs. salmon steaks 1½" thick	½ tsp. dry mustard
6 black peppercorns	1 lemon, cut into wedges
1 bay leaf	

Fill medium skillet with 1" of water and spices from above. Bring to boil. Add salmon steaks. Cover skillet, lower heat, and allow to simmer for 5 to 6 minutes or until fish begins to flake. Serve fillet with 2 Tbsp. of sauce that can be made in advance.

SAUCE:

¼ cup fat free mayonnaise	2 Tbsp. fresh basil
¼ cup plain yogurt	½ tsp. salt
1 green onion, diced	¼ tsp. pepper
1 Tbsp. fresh parsley	

Combine in a food processor or blender until well blended.

$\mathcal{A}$laska is Bear Country. These intelligent, playful and inquisitive creatures are seen most frequently in areas where the bears have grown accustomed to the viewing public. As with any form of wildlife watching, respect - not fear - is the essence of enjoying Alaska's beautiful bears.

Almond Breaded Trout with Lemon Wine Sauce

4	Cutthroat or Rainbow Trout, ½-¾ lbs., pan dressed	3	eggs
1	cup flour	4	cups milk
3	tsp. salt	•	almonds, sliced
1	tsp. black pepper	•	oil

Preheat oven to 350 degrees. Make an egg wash in a large bowl by beating eggs and milk together and set aside. In a medium bowl or plate, mix flour, salt and pepper together. On another plate, spread sliced almonds. Coat trout by placing in the egg wash, flour mixture, egg wash, then sliced almonds. Fry trout in a large skillet over medium high heat until browned on both sides. Place on baking sheet and bake for 7 to 10 minutes. Remove and serve with lemon wine sauce. May accompany with fresh steamed vegetables and sourdough bread.

LEMON WINE SAUCE:

1	cup lemon juice or lemon juice from 1 large lemon	1	Tbsp. butter or margarine
1	cup white wine	2	Tbsp. cornstarch
1	cup shallot	2	Tbsp. water
		1	tsp. parsley, chopped

Sauté minced shallot and margarine over medium heat, do not brown. Add lemon juice, wine and parsley; bring to a boil. Combine cornstarch and water. Add to hot mixture, stirring constantly until thickened. After sauce thickens, remove from heat and serve over Almond Breaded Trout.

*B*y now all the world sings the praises of delicious Alaskan salmon. King, sockeye or chum. Red, silver or pink. The salmon-rich creeks and riverways at times "run pink" or "red" with the abundance of fish - thousands upon thousands of them - swimming the icy blue waters.

Sautéed Salmon Fillets with Watercress Dill Sauce

4	salmon fillets	1	clove garlic, minced
1	tsp. salt	2	Tbsp. oil
4	Tbsp. flour	2	Tbsp. butter
½	tsp. white pepper	2	lemons, halved

Dust salmon fillets with flour, salt and pepper mixture and set aside. Heat oil and butter in a large skillet. Add minced garlic and salmon fillets and sauté together over medium heat until salmon begins to flake. Remove from heat and serve immediately. Top each fillet with chilled Watercress Dill Sauce accompanied by lemon halves.

WATERCRESS DILL SAUCE:

½	cup watercress leaves	2	Tbsp. lemon juice
¼	cup scallions, sliced	½	tsp. salt
¼	cup fresh dill, chopped	¼	tsp. black pepper
1	clove garlic, minced	2	Tbsp. oil
3	anchovy fillets, chopped	½	cup sour cream
1	cup mayonnaise		

Blend all ingredients except sour cream in a blender until smooth. Remove and fold in sour cream. Chill until ready to serve.

Scampi Style Halibut

1½	lbs. halibut, cut into 4 to 6 oz. portions	½	tsp. oregano leaves
4	large cloves garlic	⅛	tsp. salt
½	cup butter	2	Tbsp. grated Parmesan cheese
1	Tbsp. fresh lemon juice	¼	cup fresh parsley, chopped
		•	Lemon wedges for garnish

Preheat oven to 400 degrees. Place halibut fillets into bottom of a broiler pan or jelly roll pan. Melt butter, Parmesan cheese and seasonings over low heat in a small sauce pan. When melted, stir in fresh parsley. Pour over halibut and place in preheated oven for 8 to 12 minutes or until fish is flaky. Garnish with lemon wedges and parsley sprigs. Serve with fresh steamed vegetables or tossed salad along with Sourdough French bread.

Honey Mustard Halibut

1½	lbs. fresh halibut fillets	1	Tbsp. lemon juice
2	Tbsp. oil	2	tsp. vegetable salt substitute

SAUCE: COMBINE AHEAD OF TIME.

3	Tbsp. coarse brown mustard	2	Tbsp. honey
2	Tbsp. light mayonnaise	1	tsp. yellow prepared mustard

Preheat oven to 450 degrees. Place 4 servings of halibut in a single layer of a shallow baking pan sprayed with vegetable pan coating. Brush tops of fillets lightly with oil and sprinkle salt substitute seasoning on fillets. Sprinkle with lemon juice. Bake 10-15 minutes or until the thickest part of fillet flakes easily. Serve with rice and 2 Tbsp. of sauce. Yield: 4 servings.

Salmon Cheese Chowder

1	lb. salmon, cooked	1	cup cream
1½	cups onion, chopped	2	cups sharp Cheddar cheese
1½	cups celery, chopped	1	tsp. thyme, crushed
3-4	Tbsp. butter	1	Tbsp. Worcestershire sauce
4	medium potatoes, diced	2	Tbsp. fresh parsley, minced
1	cup chicken broth	•	salt & pepper to taste
3	cups milk		

Sauté onions and celery in butter until transparent and tender. Add potatoes and chicken broth and simmer about 20 minutes until potatoes are tender. Add remaining ingredients. Cook over medium heat, stirring constantly until salmon is hot and cheese is melted, being careful not to boil. Salt and pepper to taste. Garnish with parsley. Yield: 6 servings.
(Pictured on page 26)

The arctic summer...quite literally, the day never ends. Pastimes like reeling salmon, sea bass and halibut from pure Alaskan streams are enjoyed at all hours. Naturally, the natives take the phenomena all in stride. But for newcomers, the nightless days are one of the most memorable parts of an Alaskan adventure.

Salmon Dill Omelet

3	Tbsp. butter or margarine	¼	tsp. salt
1	cup flaked canned or poached salmon (boneless & skinless)	¼	tsp. pepper
		3	oz. cream cheese, softened
¼	cup onion, minced	2	Tbsp. fresh snipped dill or
5	eggs, slightly beaten		1 Tbsp. dill weed

In a 10" skillet or 8" omelet pan, melt 2 Tbsp. butter until sizzling. Add minced onion & salmon. Cook over medium heat until onions are transparent, about 3 minutes. Remove from skillet and set aside. In a small bowl, beat eggs, salt, pepper and milk until slightly frothy. In the same skillet, melt 1 Tbsp. butter until sizzling. Pour egg mixture into skillet and cook over medium heat. Lift edges and allow the liquid to run underneath until the omelet mixture is set. Dot cream cheese on the top of the omelet and place salmon and onion mixture over one half of omelet. Gently fold other half over omelet mixture. Garnish with lemon twist or fresh dill sprig. Yield: 2 servings.

 $\mathcal{W}$ ith 591,000 square miles of land, Alaska by and large is vast, unchartered territory. More than double the size of Texas, much of the 49th state remains untamed and quietly remote. No roads. No phones. No daily flights. The wild and wonderful outback awaits only the well-equipped and brave-hearted.

Stuffed Sole Fillets with Asparagus & Hollandaise

6-8	long sole fillets	1	egg, beaten
1	cup herb seasoned croutons	1	large bunch asparagus
4	Tbsp. margarine		(24 spears), blanched
¼	cup onion, diced	3	lemons, quartered
2	Tbsp. parsley flakes		*May substitute sourdough*
1	can chicken broth or		*bread for the croutons.*
	1 tsp. bouillon + 4 oz. water		

Preheat oven to 375 degrees. Wash sole fillets and pat dry and set aside. Melt margarine, add onions and cook until transparent (do not brown). Add parsley and ½ of the chicken broth and heat until hot. Remove from heat, add egg and mix well. Add croutons and gently stir until all are moistened. Cover and set aside. Clean asparagus and cut into 4" long spears; lay out sole fillets. Place ½ cup of stuffing mixture and 4 asparagus spears on each fillet. Roll up with spears being visible from sides. Place in a greased 9" X 13" baking dish. Pour other ½ of chicken broth in dish and add water if broth does not completely cover bottom. Cover with aluminum foil, being careful not to allow foil to touch the fish. Bake covered in oven for 30 minutes or until fish begins to flake. Remove from oven. Squeeze lemon juice on each fillet and serve with Hollandaise sauce over top.

The cultural offerings in Sitka are rich and diverse. Its museums of art and history are highly acclaimed. But what first beckons tourists to the city's shores is Mount Edgecombe - a snow-streaked beauty many consider to be the most glorious feature of the western horizon.

Cheddar Broccoli Salmon Bake

CRUST:

1	cup herb seasoned croutons, crushed	⅓ cup margarine

Heat margarine in a large microwave safe bowl, in the microwave until melted. Stir in crushed croutons. Press mixture into a greased 9" X 13" baking dish and set aside. Preheat oven to 350 degrees.

FILLING:

2½	cups herb seasoned croutons, crushed	3	eggs
1½	cups Cheddar cheese, shredded	1½	cups broccoli florets, washed & cut in bite size pieces
1	cup water	2	tsp. chicken bouillon or 2 bouillon cubes
¾	cup milk	1	tsp. dry mustard powder
1	lb. cooked salmon, boned & flaked	2	Tbsp. onion, minced

Mix all ingredients together thoroughly and gently spoon into baking dish. Bake for 45 to 50 minutes or until heated through. When done, remove from oven and allow to set for 10 to 15 minutes.

SAUCE:

⅓	cup margarine	½	tsp. salt
2	Tbsp. cornstarch	1½	cups fresh tomatoes, diced
1⅓	cups water	½	cup fresh broccoli, diced
1	tsp. dill weed		

Cook margarine, cornstarch, water, dill and salt in a medium saucepan; stirring constantly to a full boil. Add tomatoes and broccoli and continue cooking for 1 to 2 minutes. Remove from heat. Serve over Salmon Bake if desired.

Alaskan Style Cioppino

1-½ lbs. halibut, cut into large
     bite size pieces
20   shrimp, peeled & deveined
2   Dungeness Crab, disjointed
10   clams or mussels in shells
3   bay leaves
¼   cup olive oil
1   onion, diced
2   bunches green onions, diced
1   green pepper, diced
5   cloves garlic, minced
2   cans stewed tomatoes
2   cans Mexican style tomatoes
1   can tomato, pureé
1   cup dry white wine
3   Tbsp. fresh basil, chopped
•   salt & pepper to taste

Heat oil in a large soup or stock pot. Add onions, green onions, peppers and bay leaves. Sauté until onions are transparent. Add garlic and sauté for 2 or 3 minutes more. Add tomatoes, tomato puree and white wine. Cover and simmer for 45 minutes. Add a little water if necessary. Add salt and pepper. Remove bay leaves. Add clams or mussels and crab. Cover and simmer for about 10 minutes. Add shrimp and halibut and simmer until fish is just cooked through. Stir in chopped fresh basil. Serve immediately. Yield: 6 servings.

Classic Clam Chowder

¼   lb. bacon, chopped
1½   lbs. clams, chopped
1   lb. red new potatoes, scrubbed,
     cooked and cubed
1   large onion, chopped
¼   cup flour
2   cups milk
2   cups heavy cream
2-3 Tbsp. fresh parsley, chopped
•   salt & freshly ground pepper

Sauté the bacon and onion over medium heat until bacon is cooked. Pour off accumulated bacon fat. Now add the clams and sprinkle the mixture with the flour. Cook for about 3 minutes, stirring constantly. Add the milk and cream. Continue to stir as soup thickens. Stir in the potatoes and seasonings to taste and continue cooking just until potatoes are heated through. Serve in bowls with a dollop of butter and a sprinkle of parsley. Yield: 4 servings.

To truly appreciate Alaska is to experience Alaska. Her charms are many. From emerald forests to salmon-rich waters, to rugged tundra and mammoth glaciers, the 49th state is one that begs to be explored. Words and pictures cease to describe what nature has so splendidly created in Alaska.

Alaskan King Crab Boil

6	whole black peppercorns	3	Tbsp. mustard seed
4	cloves	1	small cinnamon stick
8	bay leaves	1	tsp. ginger
2	whole allspice	½	tsp. dill seed
1	tsp. cracked red pepper	2-3	cobs of corn, sliced
1	Tbsp. whole coriander	1	lb. Alaskan King Crab legs

Combine ingredients in a spice bag and secure well or tie in a cheese cloth. Place in a large kettle of boiling water with 2 tsp. salt. Cover kettle and boil for 5 to 10 minutes to release aroma from spices. Place Alaskan King Crab legs into boiling water. Cover and cook for 5 to 10 minutes. Remove shellfish and drop cobs of corn into boiling water for 5 to 10 minutes. Remove and place on platter with crab legs. Yield: 4 servings.

King Crab Salad

1	cup King Crab	½	cup mayonnaise
2	Tbsp. lemon juice	2	medium avocados or tomatoes
1	cup celery, finely chopped	•	crisp salad greens
½	tsp. salt		

If fresh crab is unavailable, use frozen crab meat. Flake crab meat and toss with lemon juice, chopped celery, mayonnaise and salt. Chill. When ready to serve, cut avocados in half, skin and remove seed..or..cut tomatoes in half, and remove pulp, leaving about ½" of the shell. To serve, spoon crab salad into the shells. Arrange on chilled salad greens. Yield: 4 servings.

*F*orget white sandy beaches and palm trees swaying in the breeze. For those who've experienced Alaska, images of paradise will never be the same. What's different about this place- the virgin snowfields, the Northern Lights, the prolific wildlife - is what makes it so incredibly Alaskan.

Parmesan Shrimp & Vegetables with Fettuccine

2	cups carrots, sliced diagonally	1½	tsp. salt
1	pkg. (10 to 12 oz.) Fettuccine noodles	1	tsp. lemon juice
		2	cups milk
2	cups fresh broccoli florets	½	cup grated Parmesan cheese
⅔	cup margarine	1½	lbs. steamed large shrimp, shelled & deveined
3	Tbsp. flour (heaping)		

Boil 8 cups of water in a 3 quart sauce pan. Add carrots and fettuccine. Cook over medium heat for 6 minutes. Add broccoli florets and continue to cook for 4 to 5 minutes or until broccoli is tender but still crisp. Drain in colander. Rinse with hot water and set aside. In a large pan or Dutch oven melt margarine. Stir in flour and salt. Heat to bubbling. Add milk and cook over medium heat stirring occasionally to a full boil. Boil 1 minute and turn heat to low and add shrimp and lemon juice, then fettuccine mixture. Continue cooking on low until all ingredients are heated through (about 3 to 4 minutes). Stir ½ of the Parmesan cheese into dish and sprinkle the other ½ over top of mixture. Serve immediately. Yield: 6 servings.

$\mathcal{T}$he midnight sun is characterized by its gradual fall in the north-northwest, a hovering over the horizon, and gentle rise in the north-northeast. From late spring through summer, the planet rotates on its axis tilting sunward. Amazingly, some parts of Alaska are showered with 22 hours of light on the solstice.

Scallop & Vegetable Stir-Fry with Linguine

3	Tbsp. vegetable oil		4	green onions, halved & cut 2" long
1	Tbsp. sesame oil		1	medium bell pepper, seeded & cut in 2" long julienne strips
2	cloves garlic, minced			
3	carrots, peeled, cut in 2" long julienne strips		1½	lbs. scallops, rinsed & drained
3	stalks celery, cut in 2" long julienne strips		1	pkg. linguine noodles
			2	tsp. grated ginger root or 1 Tbsp. ground ginger
1	medium zucchini, seeded & cut in long julienne strips		•	chicken or vegetable stock
½	cup medium mushrooms, halved		•	water, cold
			•	cornstarch

Combine cold water and cornstarch, set aside. In a large skillet or Wok, combine oils and garlic. Heat on high, stirring constantly until garlic begins to brown. Immediately add carrots, celery and onions, stirring constantly for about 3 minutes. Add zucchini, mushrooms, ginger, bell pepper and scallops. Continue cooking on high until scallops are white, stirring constantly. Add stock, heat to a boil, add cornstarch and water mixture and continue stirring until slightly thickened. Serve immediately over warm Linguine. Yield: 6 servings.

estled at the foot of Pioneer Peak, the Matanuska Valley is Alaska's premier agricultural region. The 100-pound cabbages and mammoth begonias are living proof of the valley's exceptionally fertile soil. Naturally, come late August, these homegrown beauties are among the blue ribbon entries at the Alaska State Fair.

Garden Vegetable Shrimp Quiche

1	deep dish pie shell (9")		¼	cup green or red pepper, diced
4	eggs, beaten		¾	cup broccoli florets
½	cup sour cream		½	cup tomatoes, seeded & diced
¼	cup milk		¼	cup mushrooms, quartered
1	tsp. salt		1	cup shrimp, peeled, deveined
½	tsp. white pepper			& cooked
¼	cup onion, diced			

Partially bake pie shell in a 350 degree oven for 5 minutes. Remove and layer onions, peppers, broccoli, tomato, mushrooms and shrimp in the pie shell. Mix eggs, sour cream, milk, salt & white pepper together in a bowl. Beat with a wire whisk for 1 minute. Pour over ingredients in the pie shell. Bake in a 325 degree oven for 20 to 25 minutes or until mixture is puffy and set. Yield: 6 servings.

Dungeness Crabmeat Bisque

5	Tbsp. margarine	2	cups milk
½	cup onions, finely chopped	2	cups heavy cream
½	cup celery, finely chopped	2	cups (1½ lbs.) Dungeness
3	Tbsp. flour		Crabmeat, freshly cooked
½	tsp. paprika		or thawed if frozen
1	tsp. salt	¼	cup dry Sherry
¼	tsp. ground white pepper		

In a large heavy saucepan, heat margarine, onions and celery. Stir constantly over medium high heat for about 5 minutes (do not brown). Add flour, paprika, salt and pepper; mix well. While stirring mixture with a wire whisk, pour milk and cream in very slowly until mixture comes to full boil and is smooth. Reduce heat to low and simmer about 3 more minutes. Add crabmeat stirring gently and heat through, about 2 or 3 minutes. Add Sherry, 1 Tbsp. at a time to desired level of flavor. Yield: 6 servings.

Cajun Style Moose Chili

1	lb. ground moose meat	2	Tbsp. chili powder
2	medium onions, diced	1	tsp. salt
½	cup green pepper, seeded & diced	¼	tsp. cayenne pepper
¼	cup Jalapeños, finely chopped	⅛	tsp. paprika
1	can (14 oz.) Mexican style tomatoes	1	can red kidney beans
2	cans (8 oz.) tomato sauce	1	can black beans, drained & rinsed
		1	cup water

Cook ground meat, onions and peppers in a large skillet until thoroughly cooked. Drain excess grease and add tomatoes, seasonings and water to meat and bring to a boil. Add beans, cover and simmer for about 1-½ to 2 hours. Quick method - cook uncovered on medium heat, stirring frequently for about 45 minutes. Yield: 4 servings.

Caribou Summer Sausage

5	lbs. trimmed caribou meat, ground fine	3	tsp. mustard seed
5	Tbsp. curing salt	1	tsp. garlic powder
3½	tsp. black pepper	1	tsp. crushed red pepper
		2	tsp. hot pepper sauce

Mix all ingredients together. Pack in casing or nylon net, tie ends with string. Refrigerate for 24 hours. Smoke for 6 to 8 hours over medium temperature. Refrigerate or freeze until ready to serve. Alternate method: Add 5 Tbsp. liquid smoke to mixture. Form sausage mixture, roll and wrap in heavy duty aluminum foil, shiny side out. Refrigerate for 24 hours. Poke holes in foil and place on rack in oven with drip pan underneath. Bake at 325 degrees for 90 minutes. Unwrap and allow to cool. Wrap in plastic wrap to store. (Pictured on page 28)

Creamy Potato Soup

¼	cup margarine	1	can (10 oz.) evaporated milk
2	cups potatoes, cubed ½"	¼	tsp. black pepper
1	cup onion, diced	¼	tsp. thyme leaves
4	cups water	½	tsp. parsley flakes
1	cup sour cream	•	salt to taste

In a soup kettle, sauté onions and margarine together until onions are transparent, not browned. Add water and potatoes and heat over medium-high heat until potatoes are tender, stirring occasionally. Add remaining ingredients and simmer for 10 minutes. Season to taste.

Parmesan Herb Biscuit Sticks

⅓	cup margarine or butter	1	cup milk
2¼	cups flour	⅓	cup Parmesan cheese
1	Tbsp. sugar	2	Tbsp. dry Herb Ranch
3½	tsp. baking powder		dressing mix
1	Tbsp. fresh parsley, chopped		

Preheat oven to 400 degrees. In a medium bowl, mix flour, sugar, baking powder and parsley. Add butter and milk; mix into a soft dough. Shape dough into a rectangle, about 12" long. Mix Parmesan cheese and dressing together. Sprinkle ½ of mixture on one side of dough. Turn over and sprinkle on other side. You may pat the dough a little to help Parmesan adhere to dough. Cut into 1" wide strips. Place onto a well buttered baking dish. Bake for 20 to 25 minutes or until lightly browned. Yield: 6 servings. *(Pictured on page 18)*

Sourdough Corn Bread

¾	cup sourdough	1	cup warm milk
1	cup flour	1	cup corn meal
¼	cup butter	¼	cup sugar
1	egg	1	tsp. salt
½	tsp. soda		

Preheat oven to 425 degrees. Mix together sourdough, milk and flour and set aside. Cream butter and sugar. Mix in egg. Add butter mixture to sourdough batter, then add cornmeal, salt and soda. Mix batter until blended. Prepare either an 8" square pan or a 9" x 13" baking pan by greasing it generously. Bake thick bread for 25 minutes and thin bread for about 20 minutes. Yield: 8 servings. *(Pictured on page 26)*
(Easy Sourdough Starter on page 31)

Sourdough Blueberry Muffins

½	cup milk	1	tsp. baking powder
1	cup sourdough starter	¾	cup sugar
	(recipe on page 31)	1	egg
¼	cup vegetable oil	½	tsp. baking soda
2	cups flour	1	cup fresh blueberries

Preheat oven to 400 degrees. Mix sourdough, milk, egg and oil together. Sift together dry ingredients and fold (do not beat) them into the liquid. Don't overmix. Dust blueberries lightly with flour and fold them into batter. Pour into prepared muffin pans and bake for about 25 minutes. Serve hot with butter. Yield: 12 muffins.

Easy Sourdough Starter

2	cups flour	1-½	cups warm water
½	tsp. yeast	3	Tbsp. sugar

Dissolve yeast in warm water and pour over remaining ingredients, stirring thoroughly. Put the lid on the pot loosely and let sit in a warm place (85 degrees). Keep the sourdough starter warm for about three days, stirring once or twice daily. It should develop a definite "sour" smell. Liquid rising to the top is normal. The sourdough is now ready to use in recipes. After using, add about 1 cup flour and 1 cup warm water to replenish. If you are not going to use the sourdough in the next day or so, store in the refrigerator, tightly covered. When planning to use, set pot in warm place, add 1 cup each water and flour, and let work overnight. Remember that many sourdough recipes use the "sponge" method, which requires you to start the recipe several hours ahead of when you want the finished product.

Rhubarb Muffins

½	lb. rhubarb, tops removed	⅓	cup nuts, finely chopped
1⅔	cups flour	⅔	cup brown sugar, packed
1	tsp. baking powder	¾	cup buttermilk
¼	tsp. grated nutmeg	⅓	cup oil
½	tsp. baking soda	1	egg, beaten
½	tsp. salt	2	tsp. vanilla extract

Preheat oven to 375 degrees. Wash rhubarb, trim off ends and dice. Mix together in a large bowl the dry ingredients and set aside. In a separate bowl, mix the remaining ingredients except rhubarb, together. Add liquid to flour mixture and stir until all ingredients are moistened. Do not over beat. Fold in diced rhubarb. Spoon batter into prepared muffin tins. Bake for 18 to 20 minutes. Cool in the pan for 5 minutes before removing. Yield: 12 muffins.

Baked Alaska Pie

18	vanilla finger cookies, split in half	½	gallon vanilla ice cream, slightly softened
⅓	cup orange flavor liqueur	¼	tsp. salt
1	pt. fresh raspberries	⅛	tsp. cream of tartar
4	egg whites, at room temperature	⅔	cup sugar

Line a 9" pie plate with ⅔ vanilla finger cookies; allow cookies to extend over the edge of the pie plate. Sprinkle with half of the liqueur. Spoon half of the ice cream over cookies. Swirl the raspberries into the ice cream and spread out evenly. Place the remainder of cookies over ice cream and cover with remaining ice cream. Sprinkle the second half of liqueur over cookies and freeze at least 4 hours or until frozen through. About 20 minutes before serving, preheat oven to 500 degrees. In a large mixing bowl, beat egg whites, salt and cream of tartar on high until soft peaks begin to form. Beat in sugar, 2 Tbsp. at a time, until sugar is dissolved and egg whites stand in stiff peaks. Spread meringue over pie, making sure to seal the edges. Swirl up in points. Bake for 3 to 4 minutes until lightly brown. Serve immediately. You may accompany with fresh raspberries. *(Pictured on page 30)*

Cranberry Orange Relish

12	oz. fresh cranberries	4	medium red apples, cored
3	medium oranges, seeded, but not peeled	4	cups sugar

Coarsely chop washed cranberries and seeded oranges in food processor or blender. Add sugar and mix thoroughly. Refrigerate overnight.
OPTIONAL: add 2 cups of miniature marshmallows and 1 cup of English walnuts just before serving, if desired. Cranberry Relish may be substituted for other fruit in muffin recipes. (Pictured on page 30)